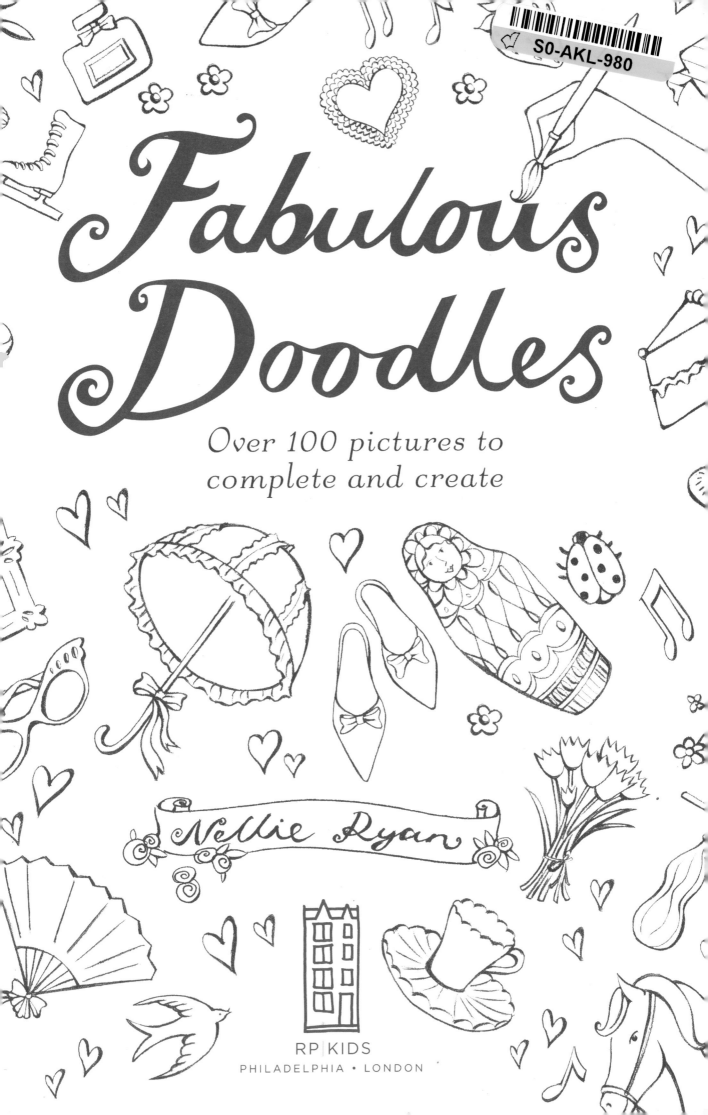

Fabulous Doodles

Over 100 pictures to
complete and create

Nellie Ryan

RP|KIDS
PHILADELPHIA · LONDON

First published in Great Britain by Buster Books,
an imprint of Michael O'Mara Books Limited, 2008

First published in the United States
by Running Press Book Publishers, 2009

Printed in China

9 8 7 6 5 4 3 2 1
Digit on the right indicates the number of this printing

ISBN 978-0-7624-3653-8

Illustrated by Nellie Ryan

This edition published by Running Press Kids,
an imprint of
Running Press Book Publishers
2300 Chestnut Street
Philadelphia, PA 19103-4371

Visit us on the web!
www.runningpress.com

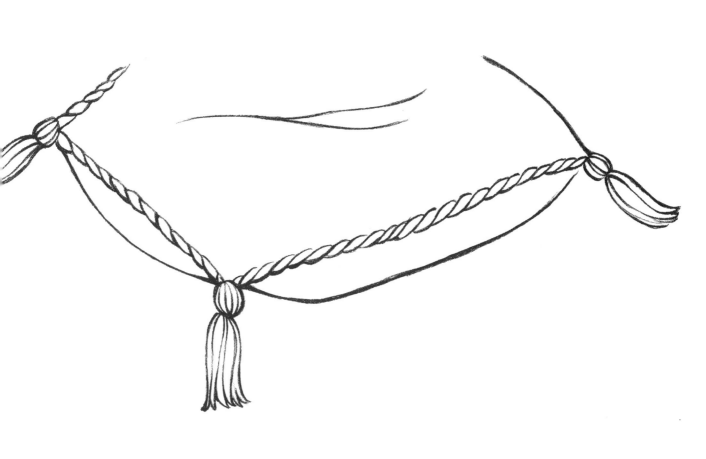

Cinderella's glass slipper.

Decorate the gypsy caravan.

Fabulous perfume bottles.

Finish the Russian dolls.

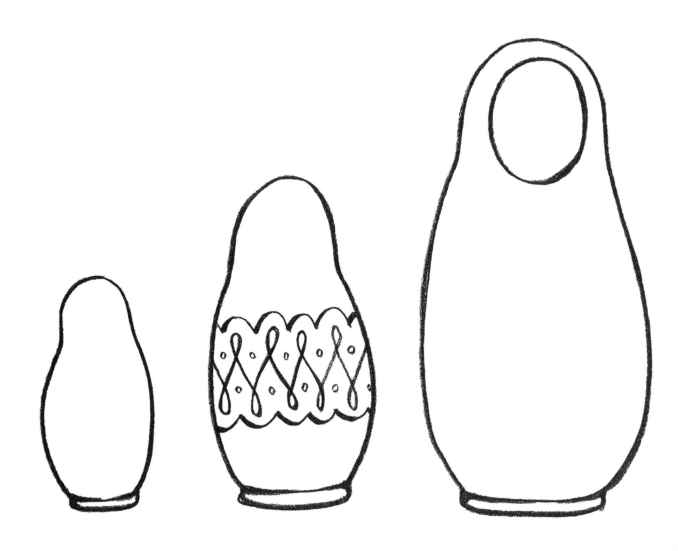

Fill the page with butterflies.

Such gorgeous gift boxes!

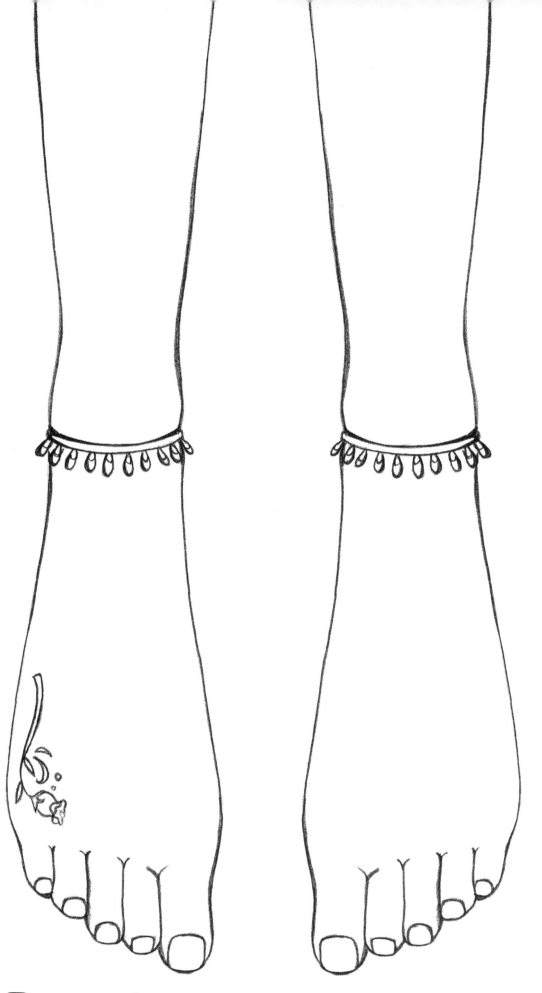

Paint her feet with henna.

Fill the stand with flowers.

What can they see down there?

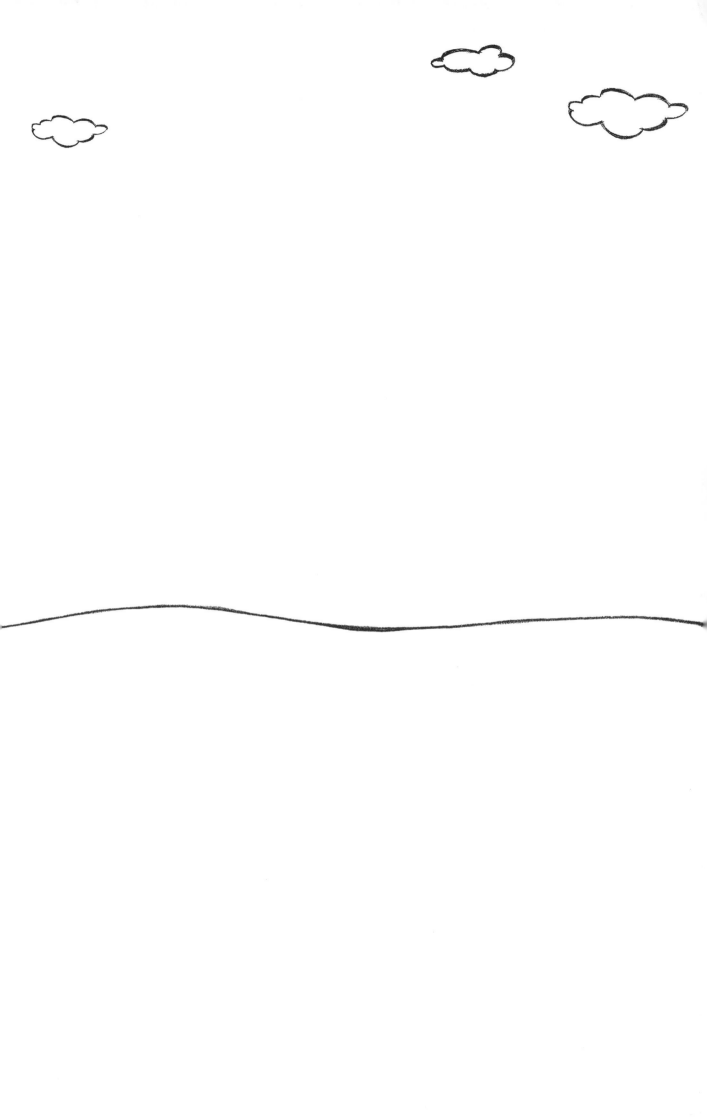

Catch it!

Buckles or bows?

Lots of beautiful rings.

Fill the page with falling leaves.

Lovely lanterns.

Grow a beautiful bonsai tree.

Create your own coat of arms.

Decorate her scooter.

What is she daydreaming about

Teepee-tastic!

What a breathtaking ball gown.

Decorate the cake.

What a gorgeous kimono!

Complete the girls' costumes.

Funk up her beach towel.

Fill the page with your favorite food.

Customize my snowboard.

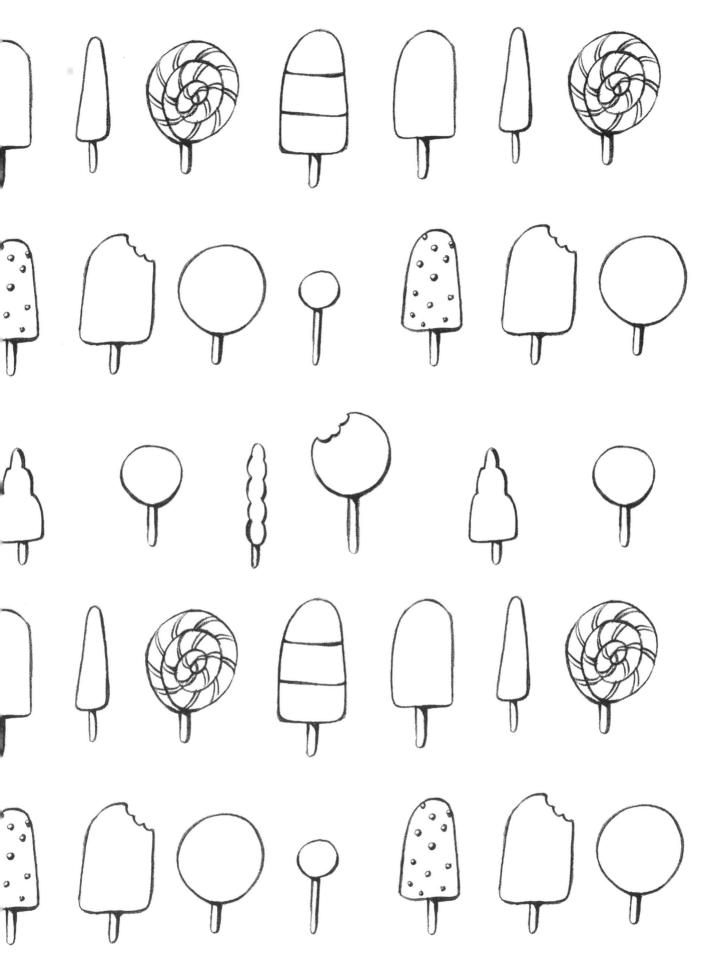

Decorate the lollipops.

Super-stylin' surfboards.

Put patterns on the teacups.

Give me a fancy collar and coat.

Finish the four-poster bed.

Hand paint these hearts.

Fill the page with flowers.

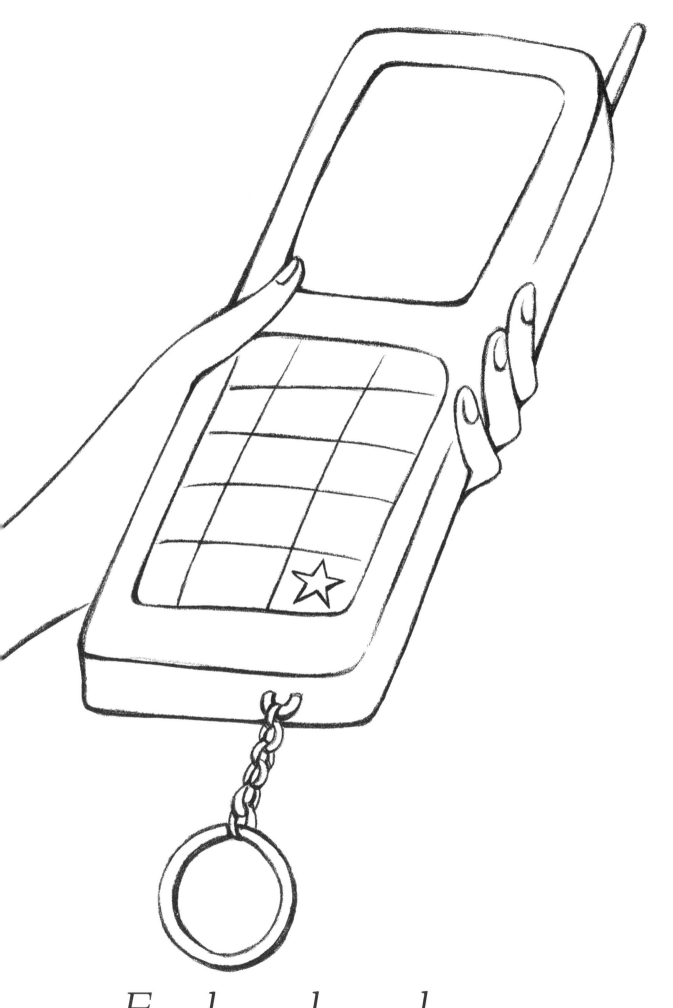

Funk up her phone.

Who is in her gondola?

Fill the box with buttons.

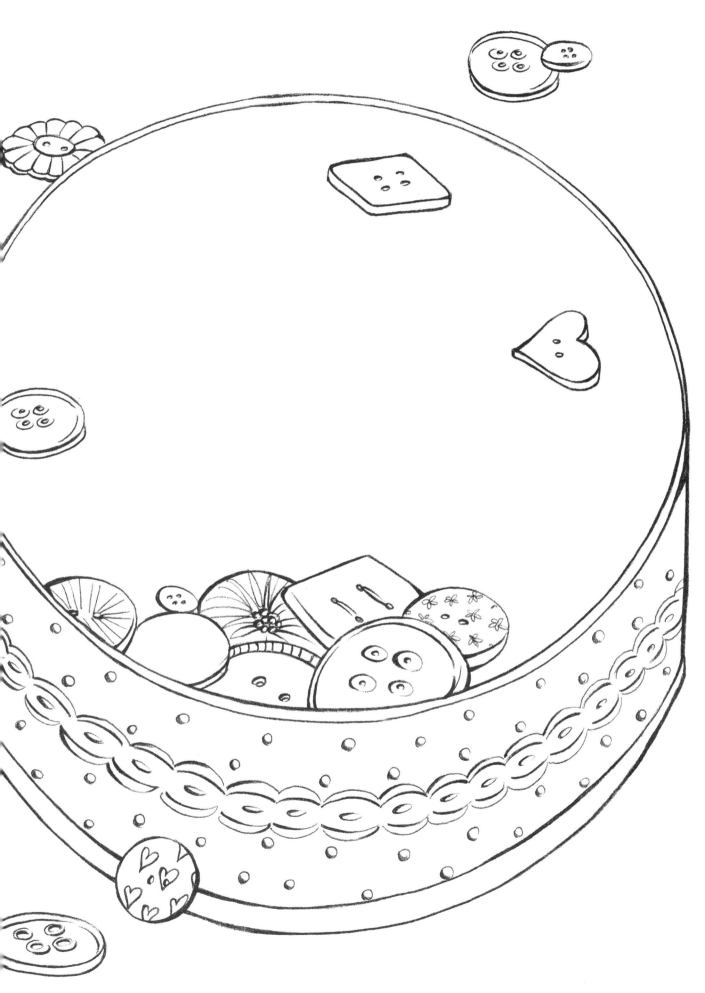

Grow the other orchids.

What an amazing ice sculpture

Draw the mermaids
at the party.

Finish the queen's costume.

Dress the pirate.

Finish the princess' carriage.

Style the horse's mane and tail

What is she pulling?

Fill the floating market.

What a beautiful bag.

Decorate the merry-go-round.

What does her limo look like?

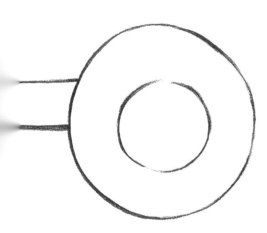

Fabulous fireworks!

What is she carrying?

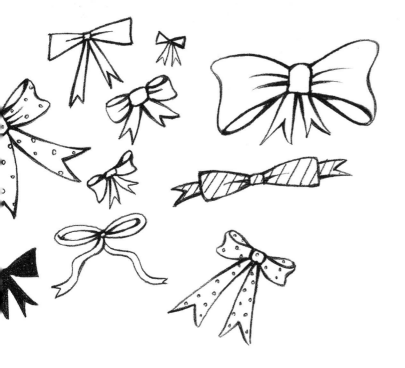

A billion beautiful bows.

Picnic time!

What is in the attic?

Who is on the red carpet?

The latest hairstyle.

Bon appetit.

What is the band wearing?

Decorate the tights.

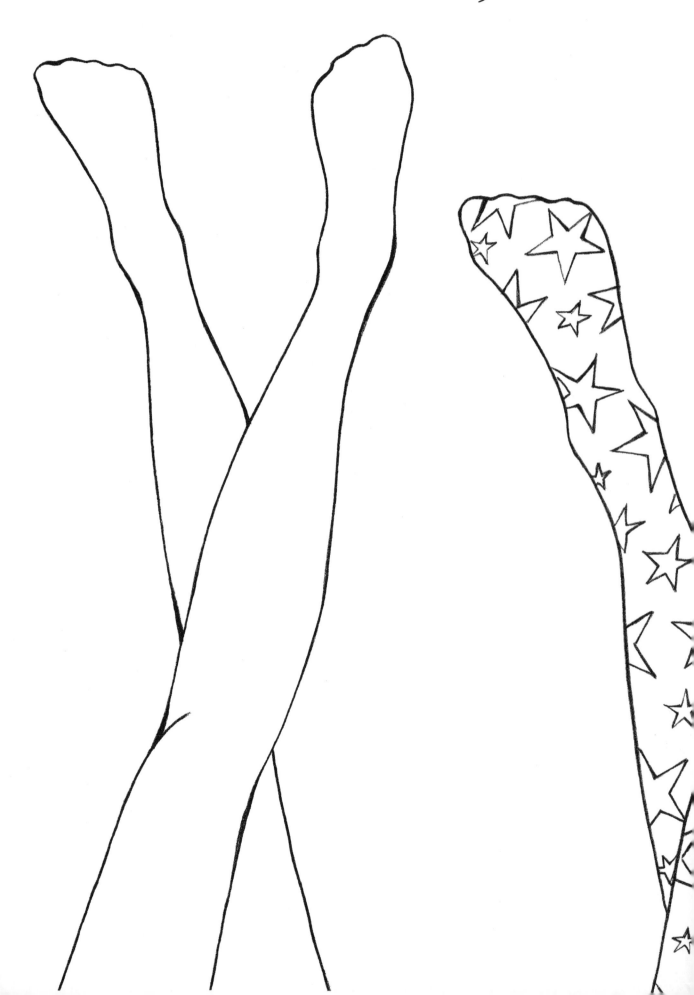

Twelve dancing princesses.

Allacazam!

Create a window display.

What a magical tent!

What is in the locket?

Where has she been shopping?

Decorate the dancer's skirt.

Customize her school uniform.

Fill her beautiful boudoir.

Decorate their masks and gown.

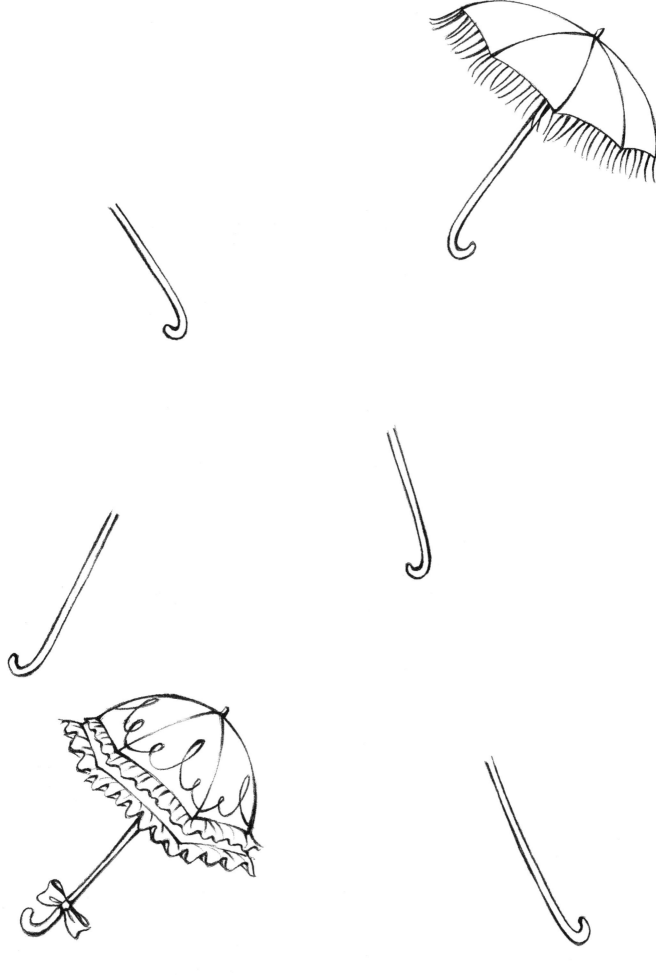

Such pretty parasols!

Add the castle's turrets.

A throne fit for a princess.

Sensational sunglasses!

Lots of love.

Design the perfect outfit.

What sensational swimsuits.

Cover the garland with flowers.

Finish the patchwork quilt.

What pretty shoes!

Ice the cookies.

What fantastic feathers!

A fire-breathing dragon.

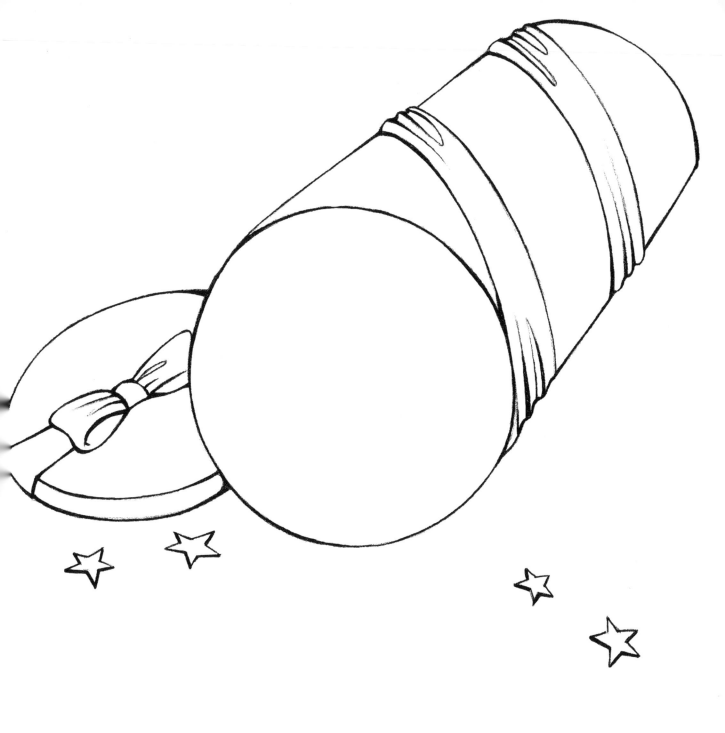

What is in the time capsule?

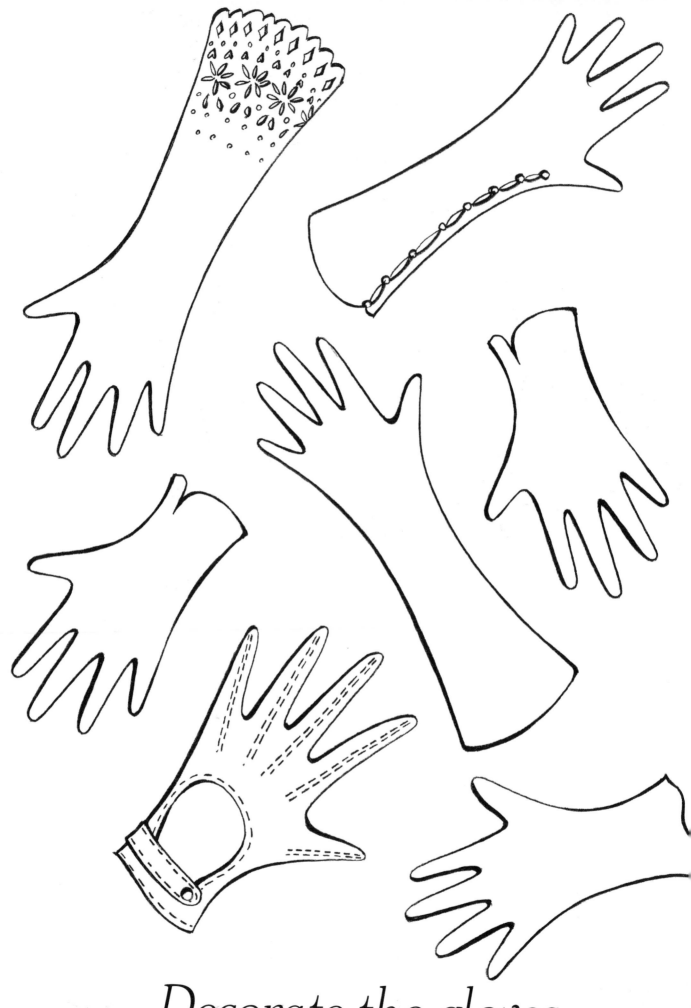

Decorate the gloves.

Design her tutu.

Paint the toy maker's toys.

Finish the fans.

Complete the chorus line's costumes.

What is growing in her garden?

Add an amazing table decoration.

Hall of mirrors.

What is the waiter serving?

Fill the shop with hats.

What amazing vases!

Where is she heading?

Give them fabulous hairstyles.

Yummy!

A beautiful fountain.

Who is riding the elephant?

Fill in her fairy friends.

Design some snazzy stationery.

Frame the mirrors.

What are they filming?

A stormy snow globe.

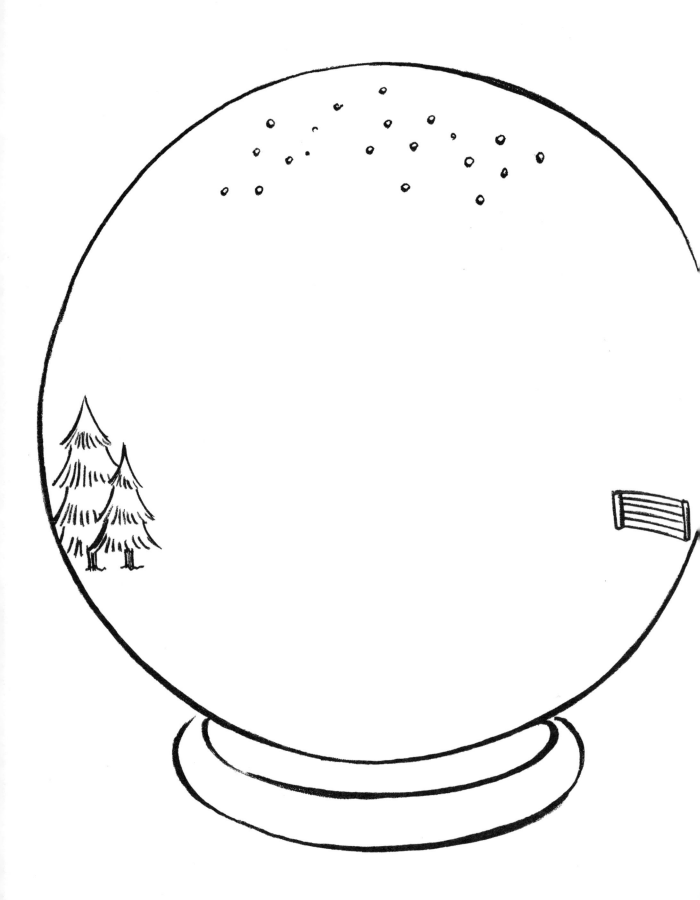